S E C R E T A

SECRETA

Three Methods of Laying Gold Leaf

By JOYCE GRAFE

OREGON HISTORICAL SOCIETY PRESS

This volume was produced by the Oregon Historical Society Press.

Library of Congress Cataloging in Publication Data

Grafe, Joyce.
Secreta: three methods of laying gold leaf / by Joyce Grafe.
p. cm.
Includes bibliographical references.
ISBN 0-87595-225-9 (alk. paper): $12.95
1. Gilding—Technique. 2. Illumination of books and manuscripts—Technique. I. Title.
[ND3327.G54G7 1990]
745.6'7'028—dc20 89-26593
CIP

First edition (limited deluxe and limited trade) published in 1985 by the Alcuin Press, Portland, Oregon. Second edition (paperback) published in 1986 by the Taplinger Publishing Co., Inc., New York, New York.

The paper used in this publication meets the minimum requirements of American National Standard for Information Sciences—Permanence of Paper for Printed Library Materials. ANSI Z32.48—1984.

Printed in the United States of America.

This book is dedicated to the medieval scribes and illuminators whose labors produced a legacy of mysteries and knowledge.

Deo Gratias.

Contents

Foreword ix
Introduction 1
Gum Ammoniac 7
Gesso 17
Hyplar 59
Egg Tempera and Glair 69
Technical Notes 79
Glossary 85
Bibliography & Resources 93

Foreword

Physician and artist often worked hand in hand in the early medieval cloister, the physician discovering, preparing and supplying the artist's pigments, as well as tending to the sick. These early physicians left a legacy of prescriptions for colors and cures which was gradually expanded over the centuries. When knowledge of art and medicine began to move from the cloister to the secular world, these collections were published by secular physicians as "Secreta," directions for the art of illumination intermingled with chemical formulae and prescriptions for common ailments. The oldest of these date from the seventh to the tenth century.[1]

The art of gilding manuscripts (the laying of gold) also changed with the passing centuries. Several successful methods were developed, ranging from the suspension of gold in glue to the use of plaster bases. In the following chapters, we will explain three methods of gilding: two very old, gum ammoniac and gesso, and one new, Hyplar.

Currently available information on the subject of gilding is instructionally vague, while books featuring facsimile works concentrate on the painting of miniatures. This book has been written to fill that instructional gap; to serve the calligrapher as well as the art historian by detailing methods for laying gold that are practiced today; and to touch upon the making and use of egg tempera and glair to mix with pigments.

Throughout the text runs a schema of black and white drawings which were made from facsimiles and reproductions of extant manuscripts of the Western European tradition. As samples they will introduce, in historical sequence, decorative techniques and stylistic devices which were integrated with the use of gold and

---

[1]W. R. Tymms and W. D. Wyatt, *The Art of Illuminating* (London, 1861), p. 45.

Foreword

1. *Book of Kells, Gospel of Matthew, ca. 800*
Enlarged detail from the base of a letter, exemplifying "interlace" or the curvilinear filling-in of space; combined with zoomorphic figures.

letterform and deserve attention, apart from miniature painting, as other components of illuminated manuscripts.

As with calligraphy, formal reproduction of traditional decorative styles develops the sense of balance necessary to effectively carry these patterns with one's own embellishments into contemporary work. Research is very important in this attempt. Styles and periods have been conveniently labelled by historians, but as is the case with other historical cataloging, these labels and demarcations are not rigid; nor do they apply simultaneously in all locations. Certain characteristics of a style may evolve more rapidly than others, some artists may take more creative liberties with traditional patterns, and advances in methods and availability of materials will vary.

It is advantageous to study examples from all periods and traditions; taking note of colors, style, date, and provenance, as well as letterform. In this effort the student will gain crucial visual *information from published anthologies and facsimiles of illuminated manuscripts. Without the proper background, the temptation to do a piece by pulling this and that from what might be appealing, in combination with a favorite alphabet, can be overwhelming. The results of combining pretty parts into such an eclectic style will not make a pretty whole.*

This volume is offered in the hope that, like the ancient "Secreta" and books of Theophilus, it will provide a clear guide for generations of illuminators to come.

Acknowledgements

NO BOOK IS WRITTEN without the support, input and consideration of people other than the author. I acknowledge those individuals now:

All the fellow calligraphers who kept insisting that I "write it down";

Larry and Angela Dworkin for their support and free computer time;

Son Rod who kept us legal, and son Marc who toiled valiantly at the computer, bringing, in the most frustrating moments, the gift of laughter;

Husband Herman, a very special man, who was confident that I could do anything, and who sympathized and took me out to dinner;

The three people who made this book a reality with their rare talents, warmth and tenacity—Jack Thompson, Elizabeth Chambers and Charles Lehman.

To you, my friends and family, I give heartfelt thanks.

Introduction

GOLD OF ITSELF has no adhesive quality. It must adhere to a material which in turn adheres to the paper or skin support. Therefore, gold is laid on a material that is called a base, which is affixed to a support. A base is either made by the artist, or it is purchased. It is then mixed, applied to the paper or vellum, allowed to dry to a certain state, and finally gold is burnished onto it. Because of its ingredients, a base will always be slightly raised from the surface of the support and, depending on the specific base, may mound-up, becoming a "raising base."

The three bases discussed in this book are presented in their historical order of appearance. Gum ammoniac, a resinous gum, and gesso, a plaster-based size, have been in use for centuries. Hyplar, which is a commercially prepared petroleum product, is a modern material. Each is employed for the same purpose, to affix gold to a surface, and each method produces a different effect. In general, the bases are all handled in the same way. Included in this introduction are a series of exercises (PRACTICING WITH BASES) which should be referred to in conjunction with each of the methods for laying gold. Egg tempera and glair have merited a chapter due to their historical role in manuscript production and because, when mixed with watercolor, a brilliant and extremely durable color results. The techniques for using egg tempera and glair are presented with instructions for making a color wheel which will give the artist facility in managing the various mixtures of color, and a handy reference for future design work.

In approaching illumination there is an order to be followed which will help in avoiding setbacks: calligraphy, gilding, and lastly, painting. This helps to protect the artist from the misspelled word, as well as technical problems arising from trying to lay gold after the painting.

Before selecting a base, one of the first steps to consider is the transfer of a completed design to the support of paper or skin. All design work should be executed on tracing paper. The back of the paper is then graphitized and the design is traced, copying it onto the support. Complete instructions for design transfer may be found in the Technical Notes section.

After the design, the concern must be with the support itself. Familiarity with both paper and skin is important, as they lend themselves to the display and preservation of illumination in different ways.

2. *Book of Kells, Gospel of Luke, ca. 800*
a) & b) Zoomorphic initials.

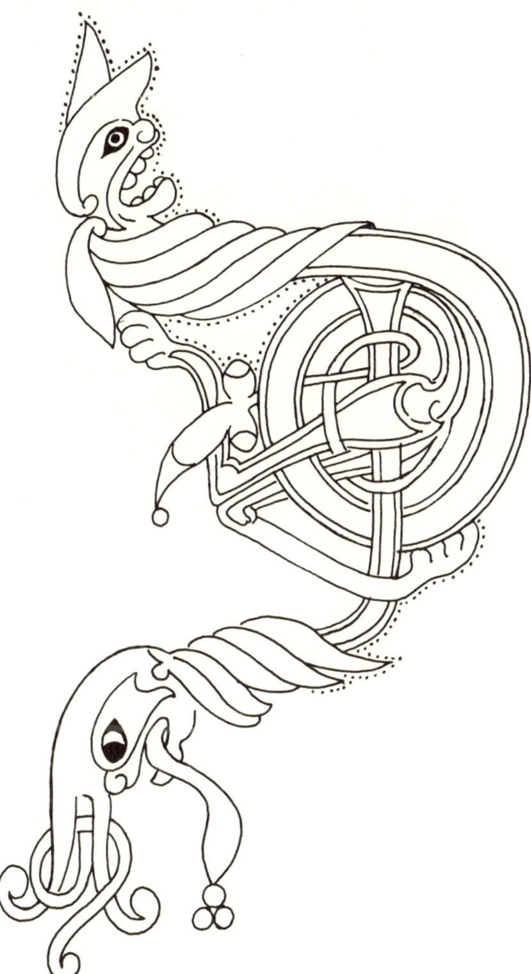

For practicing with bases I recommend a coated paper of heavy substance with a smooth surface to give gold its best appearance. (Bond paper or other paper of similar weight is unsuitable.) With experimentation the student will discover the qualities which different surfaces impart and learn which combinations will lead to a desired effect. For "finished" work use 100% rag content paper with a low or neutral pH factor. Papers with a high acid content begin to disintegrate after a few years' exposure to light and air. (Be sure to check the acid content. Papers described as 100% rag may not be acid free.)

Gilding the base requires the use of gold leaf, the varieties of which are described in detail in the Technical Notes. One type of gold that is listed, but not covered by the text, is shell gold. Shell gold may be used to highlight, or it may be painted with in the same fashion as water color and can be burnished.

PRACTICING WITH BASES

For the most part, the specific materials and techniques needed for the laying of gold will be unfamiliar. It is important to practice with them in order to gain facility, and the best practice is the filling in of geometric figures. Using a brush to fill in circles, squares, triangles, half moons (crescents), and frame-type borders provides experience in covering large areas, managing edges, and completing points of corners.

All bases are put down using the "puddle-pull" technique. This simply means that the base is applied to the support as a small puddle and with short strokes the base is carefully pulled from the puddle. The base should be kept to an even thickness. Each succeeding puddle is then placed to join the pulled strokes, overlapping them. When covering a large area, watch that the edges remain wet so that each new addition will bond seamlessly with the last.

Certain problems will quickly be encountered when you outline geometric figures and begin to fill them in. Specific remedies for these special situations are:

1. *A design with no beginning or end* (such as a circle or a square border) is best approached in this way: Pick a spot to begin and lay the base brushed thinly for about 1/4". Proceed to puddle-pull around the border. Upon reaching the spot where you

3. *Ebo Gospel, St. Matthew, Reims (France), Carolingian Empire, ca. 816-835*
Initials L & I with decorative interlace pattern.

began, feather the base lightly over the 1/4" of thin base. When the base is dry, the join will not be seen.

2. *Points of corners* are approached by puddling the base in a corner very near its point. Then pull the base into the point with the tip of the brush.

3. *Covering a large surface* presents the problem of keeping the working edge of the base wet as you move across it. At some point the base will be drying slightly on one side before you can return to it with fresh base. By alternately working towards the center, first from one outside edge, then from the other, joining the two as they meet, the problem will be minimized.

4. *The outer edge of a design* is made by pulling from a puddle to the edge, rather than making the edge first and pulling away from it.

Chapter One
GUM AMMONIAC

IMPORTED from the Middle East, gum ammoniac is often mixed with seeds, dirt and tiny twigs. Soaked, strained and tinted to make it visible, it is laid or written with brush or pen. Gum ammoniac is considered a flat base, as it is less raised than gesso or Hyplar. As a base for gilding it has been in use at least as long as gesso. Gum ammoniac is gilded with patent gold to produce a specific visual effect. Simple to use and rapid to work with, gum ammoniac offers a textured finish unlike the brilliant mirrored sheen of gesso and Hyplar. Used as a second base for gold in a design, the contrasting finish is striking.

TO MAKE GUM AMMONIAC SOLUTION

You will need:

1-2 Tbl. gum ammoniac. Depending on how much you wish to make.

3 small jars. 3 or 4 oz., one with an airtight lid (baby food jars are good).

Scissors

4 pieces clean nylon hosiery. Cut the leg tube open, then cut into approx. 7" lengths (Dynel or fine silk can also be used.)

Red watercolor

Finger cots or surgical gloves

Flat wooden toothpicks

Distilled water

1. Place gum ammoniac in one of the jars.

2. Add just enough water to barely cover the gum ammoniac. Close the jar with the lid and set aside to soak for 24 hours. The gum must soften. If the gum has soaked for 12 hours, the process may be hurried by placing the jar in a pan of warm water that reaches about an inch up the jar. Put the pan over very low heat to warm the gum solution until it is *just warmed through*, about 5 to 10 minutes. Use only very low heat. *Do not boil.* Remove the jar from the

8

4. *Gospels, Fleury Monastery (near Tours), Carolingian Empire, ca. 820*
Decorative framing devices are arches, commonly associated with Byzantine influences in art and architecture.

water and proceed.

An alternate method after the 12-hour soak is to put the open jar in a microwave oven for 10 to 15 seconds, or until warm.

3. With your finger (in a finger cot), mash the gum around in the liquid to get all the juice out of the gum. The liquid will now be very milky in appearance.

4. Poke a double thickness of nylon part way into a second jar. Strain the solution through the nylon into the jar, rubbing it to remove all of the liquid from the gum. (A messy, smelly, sticky business.) The residue may be saved, dried and fresh gum added at a later time for another batch; or you can discard it along with the nylon.

5. With the remaining double thickness of nylon, strain the liquid into the third jar. Discard the nylon and residue.

6. Pick up just enough watercolor with the large end of a toothpick to tint the solution a pale pink (so it can be seen) and stir it into the base. It is now ready for use.

The base should be thin enough to flow through a pen but retain a slight viscous quality. If too much water has been added in soaking the gum, the base will be too thin and will not receive the gold when it is applied. To correct this, leave the jar open to the air for a few hours, or overnight. If it is still too thin, leave it out longer. If too thick, add water to thin.

TO APPLY GUM AMMONIAC SOLUTION

You will need:

Gum ammoniac solution

Prepared design. A final design transferred to the selected surface, gone over with diluted, waterproof ink, and pencil marks erased. (See "Paper, Tracing" in

Technical Notes.)

Large piece of smooth safety glass. (17" x 22" x 1/4") taped around the edges to prevent injury to you and your surroundings.

Brush and/or pen

Magnifying glass

1. Stir the gum solution thoroughly. (The end of a brush handle is convenient for this.) Have the paper or skin flat on the large piece of smooth glass.

2. Using a brush, apply the solution wherever you want it by making a small puddle of the base and *pulling* the base from the puddle. Make another small puddle to connect with the pulled strokes and pull from it, continuing in this manner until the area is covered. (See PRACTICING WITH BASES on Page 4.) As you repeat the puddle-pull process, keep the thickness of the base even. The paper, or skin, will absorb moisture from the base and wrinkle or buckle. This will mostly disappear as the moisture evaporates. Wash out your brush or pen with distilled water as soon as the base has been put down. Gum ammoniac is also a cement, so failure to clean up promptly may cause the loss of brush and nib if it is allowed to dry. Whenever it is possible, work with a magnifying glass in one hand in order to continually check the coverage.

Gum ammoniac is a delightful medium to use with a pen. Watch carefully that each stroke of the pen carries enough of the solution so it will readily accept the gold.

3. Let the base dry for 20 to 30 minutes before checking it for readiness to gild. Once ready there is a grace period, in dry weather, of about 2 hours before the base becomes too dry to gild. In times of pro-

5. *Benedictional of Robert Jumieges, Winchester, England, 990-1037*
Bold, heavy border patterns: acanthus leaves which appear repeatedly in different periods of illumination styles; sometimes painted, sometimes gilded; sometimes a foliated vine, but always stylized.

longed high humidity you may have as long as 3 or 4 days. The base should be just past the tacky stage when you begin to test. (See "To Test the Base Before Gilding" in Step 2 below.)

TO GILD GUM AMMONIAC

There is a sequence of steps to be followed when illuminating. They must be performed in order: first, calligraphy; second, gilding; and third, painting. The reasons for this become painfully clear when the consequences of working out of sequence are considered. If, for instance, the painting has been completed before the gilding, then gold will be either pushed into the paint or swept onto it when the excess is brushed off, or both. The gold will remain in the paint. It cannot be removed; it must be repainted. Or if the gilding and painting are finished and an error is then made in the calligraphy, the artist has the pleasure of doing it all over again. Given that the calligraphy is finished and the work is resting on a level surface, then it is time to apply base.

You will need:

Large piece of smooth safety glass

Glassine paper. The package that encloses gold leaf is usually glassine paper. The size is nice to work with but you may prefer a slightly larger piece.

Patent gold. Also called transfer gold or "gold-on-tissue." Cut (including the tissue) into pieces with clean, sharp scissors, or use in the whole sheet.

Scissors. Six-inch size works well.

Skin or paper with gum ammoniac laid on the design.

Plastic straw. A drinking straw with 2-3 inches cut off of the end.

Scratch pen
Sharpened pencil-ink eraser
Large, soft brush
Magnifying glass
Prepared design. A final design, etc. . . .

1. Have the glass centered to the body; glassine paper, scratch pen and burnisher to the right of the glass; straw and magnifying glass to the left; and gold on tissue at the top. (If you are left handed, reverse these instructions.)

2. To test the base before gilding: blow through the straw onto the base with air from the throat, not the mouth. Immediately put a piece of the gold-on-tissue on the base and cover it with the glassine paper. Burnish on top of the glassine with a medium pressure. Remove the glassine and tissue; gold will remain on the base; replace the glassine and burnish again. If the base adheres, leaving a sticky spot on the tissue or glassine, or it simply sticks, then the base is still damp. Allow it to dry more before continuing.

3. When the base tests ready to receive the gold, proceed by holding the gold-on-tissue in the left hand, glassine paper in the right, and the straw in your mouth. Breathe warmly onto the work through the straw. The base may fog a bit, but do not expect it. Immediately put the gold over the spot, tissue side up, and cover it with the glassine paper. Pick up the burnisher with the right hand and burnish on top of the glassine with medium pressure. Lift off the glassine and the tissue. Some of its gold will be left behind. Replace the glassine and burnish again. Remove it and brush off the excess gold with a large soft brush. Inspect with the magnifying glass for coverage.

4. Repeat these steps until all the base is completely covered with gold. At this point the gilding is complete.

5. Clean off the excess gold with the large soft brush, using the sharpened pencil/ink eraser to remove gold that sticks to the paper, and to clean around the edges. To clean up uneven edges use a scratch nib in a pen holder turned so that the front of the nib is against the edge of the gold. (For a right-handed person the edge being worked should always be on the left, enabling you to pull against the gold with the front of the nib.) With very short strokes pull carefully against the gold while drawing the nib towards you at the same time, turning the design as you progress so that

6. *Park Bible, Meuse Valley (Romance speaking area in German Empire), ca. 1148*
Full-page initial "S."

the nib is always being pulled toward your body while pressing against the design. As you move along the edge will be cleaned, leaving no sharp edges. (Fig. 1.) Do not dig into the ground any more than is necessary.

Gilded gum ammoniac has an entirely different effect than gilded gesso or Hy-plar. The finish is not as bright, having a somewhat duller, or muted, appearance. That is one of the main reasons for its use. It also provides contrast when used as a second base in a design. However, glass gold may be substituted for patent. It will retain a high polish, but is difficult to manage. To do so, burnish the gold down with the glassine as you would with patent gold but then remove the glassine and burnish very lightly directly on the gold. Be careful; it is easy to smear the base and remove the gold already laid.

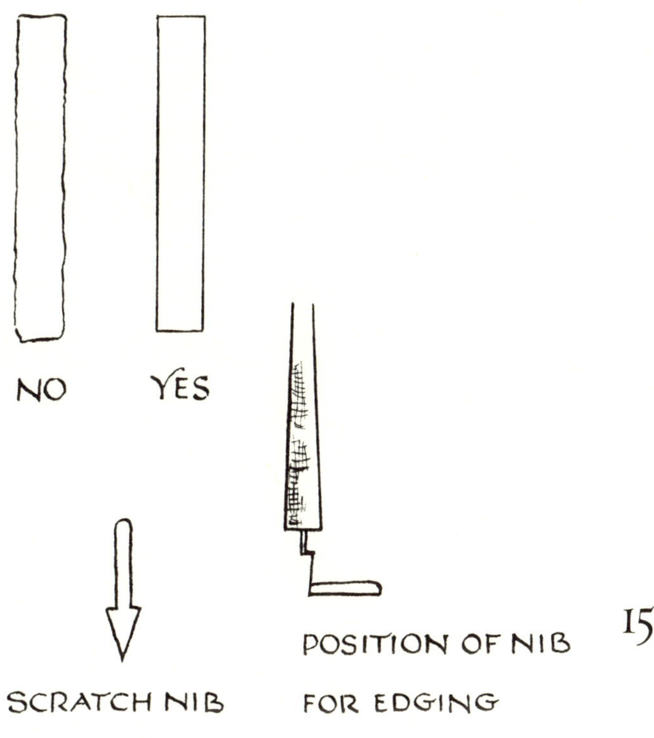

Figure 1. *Edging.*

Chapter Two
GESSO

GESSO, in today's usage, denotes a base consisting of slaked plaster (*gesso sottile*), white lead, fish glue, sugar, and Armenian bole. It is a "raising base" for the laying of gold, built up above the surface of the paper or vellum. Raised bases have been in use for centuries. In the twelfth century, Theophilus wrote of mixing glue and powdered gold, then applying it to a vellum surface prepared with a base of minium, cinnabar, and the white of an egg. The glue and gold mixture would dry slightly raised and was then burnished with a bloodstone (hematite) or a tooth. His approach sounds reasonable until you envision a room containing a contraption milling gold to a powder, a sturgeon's bladder simmering merrily on the stove for glue, and then, what about that tooth?

Historically, the constituents of gesso have been selected because of their unique qualities. White lead gives bulk, polish and malleability; sugar is hygroscopic (absorbs and retains moisture) and gives elasticity; slaked plaster gives bulk and strength; Armenian bole (jeweler's rouge) is also hygroscopic and gives color and polish; fish glue is an adhesive and acts as a binder for the medium.

Learning to use gesso requires practice and persistence. Since heat, cold and humidity affect the adhesion of gold to gesso, the weather at the time of use becomes all important. The ideal conditions combine high humidity with moderate temperatures. When attempting to work at a time of low humidity (normally a "no-go" situation), and waiting for more favorable conditions is impossible, it helps to put the work in the refrigerator, or in a cool basement, overnight. Humidifiers in the working area can be an aid, but may have detrimental effects if you are working on skin, as skin absorbs moisture in the air, frequently seizing up and cockling.

The gesso recipe found in this chapter works well in the rainy, temperate climate of Western Oregon. If in first trying this recipe the gold will not adhere under the best of conditions, adjustments may have to be made in the glue and sugar proportions, to compensate for local climatic conditions.

The tools employed for grinding, applying, and gilding the base must be *completely* free of any dirt or oil. Scrub them well with soap and water, and rinse them thoroughly several times before drying. Fog them with your breath and rub dry again using clean soft cotton cloth or soft paper towels. Any oil remaining on the tools that comes into direct contact with the gold leaf will cause it to stick and tear apart. Such mangled gold cannot be recovered for use. Keep your hands off the working ends of the clean tools.

During the polishing process, the burnisher will require constant attention. Fog it often with your breath, rubbing it firmly with a clean soft cotton cloth or a clean soft paper towel. Never continue to burnish when the burnisher sticks or hesitates; it may have picked up foreign material, or have gesso on it. The gesso itself may have become too soft with excessive blowing and require less pressure with the burnisher.

THE PREPARATION OF GESSO

You will need:

Large piece of smooth safety glass (17" x 22" x 1/4"). Sandblasted to a rough finish and taped around the edges to prevent injury

7. *Manuscript by Sarvalo of St. Armand, Valenciennes, ca. 1160*
Full-page letter A (dam) displaying intricate use of interlace interspersed with bird, animal, human figures all framed by a Greek key design.

to you and any surfaces with which it comes in contact.

Glass muller. To grind the gesso mixture.

1 or 2 spatulas. The best sizes measure 1½" to 3" across the working end (those made from bone are especially nice).

1 small metal spatula. Used only for scraping up the finished mixture and placing it on a flat surface to dry.

Measuring spoon. Used as the "part" measurement throughout the recipe (1/4 or 1/2 teaspoon is good to start with).

Flat surface. Mat board will do nicely, covered with aluminum foil, shiny side up.

Gesso sottile, 8 parts. (See Technical Notes for full recipe of *gesso sottile* and manufacturing process.)

White lead, 3 parts. WARNING: THIS IS A CUMULATIVE POISON. Wash hands thor-

oughly after using. Do not swallow it or breath its dust. Keep brush tips *out of your mouth*.

Rock sugar, 1 to 2 parts

Armenian bole, pinch to 1/2 part

Fish glue, 1 to 1-1/2 parts

Distilled water

Surgical gloves. To protect the hands and minimize direct contact with white lead.

Have ready, on a stable surface, the glass, glass muller, measure, spatulas, water and ingredients. To protect yourself, wear the surgical gloves while grinding.

Follow these steps:

1. Break up some of the *gesso sottile* onto the surface of the glass. Grind it with the muller to a very fine powder; then grind some more. Measure out the amount of plaster called for in the recipe, leveling each measure with a spatula. Place each measure on the upper left corner of the glass. (Fig. 2: set-up for making gesso.)

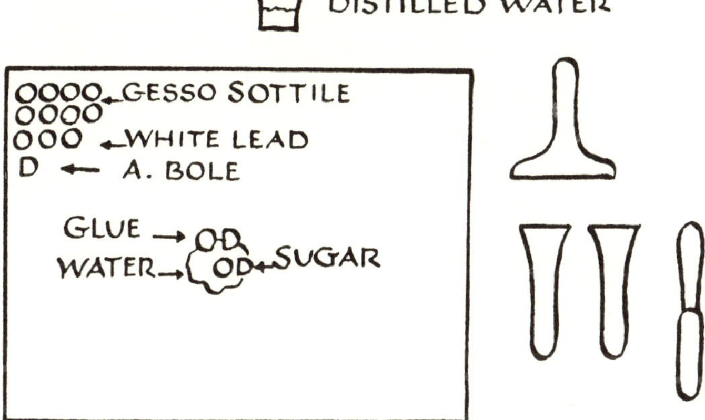

Figure 2. *Set-up for making gesso. Glass muller, bone spatulas and metal spatula at right.*

8. *Evangillary of Ste. Chappelle, Paris, 1255-60*
Letter I used as a frame for miniatures; dragon tails become decorative border devices.

Store any *gesso sottile* that is left over in a covered container. Use distilled water to wash the muller, spatula, and glass. Wipe dry.

2. Place some of the white lead on the *clean* glass and grind as above. (It is already powdery and will not require much grinding.) Repeat the directions for grinding, measuring, cleaning up, and storing. *Heed the white lead warning on page 20!*

3. Place some rock sugar on the clean glass. Grind to a very fine powder. Repeat the grinding, measuring, clean-up, and storage process.

4. Measure bole and put it with the other measures.

5. Measure glue and put it in the center of the clean glass.

9. *Choir Book, Florence, ca. 1300*
An historiated capital, the miniature (not shown) reflects the Christmas music text; flowers and acanthus weave the border.

10. *Grey-Fitzpayn Hours, England, ca. 1300-1308*
Decorative left border drops from historiated capital to include smaller illuminated letter, to a drollery at the lower margin; (I distinguish drolleries from the text-related margin painting and from grotesques which are not free standing figures but rather grow from one form into another). Right border intersperses family heraldic shields with more common birds and animals.

6. With the spatula pull the sugar into the glue; pour a measure, or possibly more, of distilled water onto the mixture. Mix it up until the sugar is dissolved.

7. Pull a portion of the remaining ingredients into the glue mix, adding more water to keep it well moistened, and begin to grind with the muller, using strong pressure.

Keep adding water by drops or spoonfuls, as appropriate, to maintain a wet but not runny consistency while grinding. (The plaster will absorb it rapidly.) The muller will quickly gather blobs which will prevent proper grinding, and must be cleaned frequently throughout the grinding process. Keep the grinding contained within a circular area on the glass about 14" in diameter. Using the spatula to scrape the base together frequently will prevent its spread over the entire glass. This simplifies clean-up and minimizes the loss of base, some of which will be lost anyway due to the rough working surface.

Gradually pull in the remaining ingredients. Continue grinding with firm pressure, adding water as needed, for 15 minutes, maintaining a strong pressure on the muller.

8. Carefully scrape the gesso together and transfer it to the upper right corner of the glass. Clean the soiled glass with distilled water.

9. Pull half of the mix back to the center. Regrind 15 minutes and move it to the left of the glass. Grind the second half of the mix 15 minutes and then pull the first half back, joining the entire mixture. Grind for 10 minutes and scrape together.) If any white specks of plaster are still evident, continue grinding until they disappear. At

11. *Queen Mary's Psalter, England, 1310-1320*
Another example of an historiated letter showing geometric pattern background for miniature; as well as grotesques, drolleries and another common vine border pattern: ivy.

this point the gesso should have a consistency similar to interior enamel house paint.

10. With the small metal spatula, drop the gesso onto the prepared foil covered surface in approximate 1" patties. Put them in a safe place to dry. This generally takes one or two days.

11. As soon as the patties are dry, remove them from the foil; they literally peel off. Store them in an airtight container. The gesso is ready for use after one week, and will store indefinitely.

TO APPLY GESSO

At this point a brief comment on general illumination procedure: first, calligraphy; second, gilding; third, the painting. If the painting has been completed before the gilding, then gold will either be pushed into the paint or swept onto it when the excess is brushed off, or both. The gold will remain in the paint, necessitating repainting. If the calligraphy is saved for the last, a mistake will mean starting over. So, with the work resting on a level surface, and the calligraphy accomplished, you are ready to apply base.

You will need:

Prepared design A design transferred to the selected surface, which has been gone over with diluted waterproof ink, and has had all pencil marks erased. (See "Paper Tracing" in Technical Notes.)

Large piece of smooth safety glass (17" x 22" x 1/4")

Cake of gesso

Shot glass. The type ordinarily used for serving a "shot" (1½ oz.) of whiskey. Short enough so the bottom can easily be reached with a finger.

Eye dropper

Toothpicks

Magnifying glass

Distilled water

Scratch nib and holder

Sharpened pencil/ink eraser

Snap-blade knife such as one made by Olfa; or a quill knife

Quill pen or pen holder with a Brause #66EF nib, or a fine nib with a very springy point.

Brush. #0 Grumbacher Series #178 or Winsor Newton 233 #1

Large soft brush

"Slip" sheet. Piece(s) of paper protecting the art not in the immediate work area

1. Break up the gesso into the shot glass, pulverizing it as much as possible. (Due to weather conditions, the cake may become quite pliant or very brittle. This does not affect its use.) With the eyedropper add two or three drops of water. Strike the bottom of the glass on a hard surface so the gesso moves and becomes dampened by the water. Set aside for 30 to 45 minutes.

2. After the gesso has soaked, using your finger (protected from the white lead by a finger cot), pack the gesso firmly into the bottom of the glass. This helps to remove air bubbles. (It will feel like semi-dry clay.)

3. Add two or three drops of water to the gesso. With a finger placed against the inside of the glass, and reaching into the *bottom*, slowly *turn the glass* and commence mixing the water and gesso together, maintaining pressure against the side of the glass. This method prevents an excess of air bubbles from forming as you blend. (Do not lift the mixing finger in and out of the glass; that will cause bubbles to develop.) At first it will be lumpy and hard to blend. Gradually add more water, a drop

at a time, and continue mixing until the consistency is slightly thicker than unwhipped cream.

With the gesso mixed, the final step in preparation is to remove any air bubbles that have developed. Use the magnifying glass to inspect the base. If there are bubbles, an authentic remedy from a 15th century illuminator is to put a finger in your ear, gather some earwax (cerumen), and stir it gently in the mix. If this ancient maneuver is unsuccessful the bubbles can be pulled out with a brush. Sometimes just letting the mix sit helps. It is extremely important to remove all the bubbles because when they dry they pop, leaving a hole in the base.

Remember you have been handling white lead, a cumulative poison. *Wash your hands thoroughly!*

4. With your work on the large, smooth piece of glass, and a magnifying glass in hand, apply gesso to a clean vellum or paper surface using a quill, brush, or pen. As a rule, the pen is used for writing with the base and the brush for covering large areas; if the pen is used to outline, the edges will be neater. When employing a brush do not push it into the gesso, as it causes air bubbles. Just dip it; *do not paint* with it. The gesso should be puddled and then pulled with the brush, very carefully, keeping the gesso layer an even thickness: do not allow thin spots to develop. (This is called the puddle-pull technique.) When applying gesso to an area that is large, watch that the edges remain wet as you progress so that each new brushful bonds seamlessly with the last. (See PRACTICING WITH BASES on Page 4.) Since the heavy elements will settle to the bottom of the

glass, stir the base every time the pen is dipped with a pen or toothpick. Gesso dries quickly and will cake the brush or pen. Clean them often with water as you work. Be sure that any excess water is removed from the brush or pen so that the base is not diluted.

5. As the gesso is drying you may discover that the base has developed valleys or dimples caused by applying the base in an uneven thickness, or tiny specks where the paper shows through. When the gesso has

12. *Hours of Jeanne d'Evreaux, France, early 14th c.*
Jean Pucelle, illuminator
An illuminated capital (not textually related); use of grotesques, drolleries, and sentence bars, here animated, sometimes geometric which visually balance a page, and function to fill out a line when the writing does not reach the designated right margin.

dried, you may add more base to these areas.

6. When the gesso is completely dry it will be necessary to do some housekeeping where the quill or brush did not leave clean edges, or a spot was patched. Use a scratch nib in a pen holder turned so that the front of the nib is against the edge of the gesso. (Fig. 1.) For a right-handed person the edge being worked should always be on the left, enabling you to pull against the gesso with the front of the nib.

Carefully, with very short strokes, pull against the gesso while drawing the nib toward you at the same time. As you move along, the edge will be cleaned and leave no sharp edges. (Fig. 1.) Do not dig into the working surface of the skin or paper any more than is necessary.

Lightly scrape the surface of the gesso with the knife to even and smooth any areas that are irregular, especially where any defects have been repaired. (Fig. 3.)

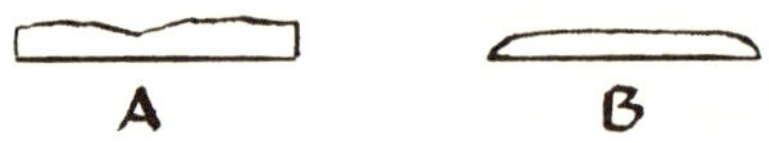

A. Unedged—rough top
B. Edged and smoothed

Figure 3. *Cross-section of gesso after smoothing and edging.*

Clean up your work as you go, using the large soft brush to sweep away any plaster bits you have trimmed.

Always have a slip sheet under your hand and arm, leaving only the immediate work area exposed. This will protect the art from irreparable accidents.

TO GILD GESSO

You will need:

Large smooth safety glass

Glass gold
Gilder's cushion
Gold-cutting knife
Hematite burnisher
Tweezers
Plastic drinking straw
Silk square
Magnifying glass
Large soft brush
Scratch pen

Always gild with the vellum or paper resting on a smooth, safety glass surface. The glass should be centered to the body with the tools placed in the following fashion (if you are left handed reverse

13. *Hours of Jeanne de Navarre, France, ca. 1350-60*
Borders embellished with birds and vines of ivy; use also of decorative background for miniature painting, drolleries and grotesques.

these directions): to the left of the glass, the straw, tweezers, and magnifying glass; to the right, the silk square, burnisher, large brush and scratch pen; at the top, the gilder's cushion and gold cutting knife.

There is a rhythm to laying gold which is the same for all bases. If you get it down, right from the beginning, you will not waste time, gold, or tearing of hair. Keep these words in mind as you gild—"Blow, Press, Burnish"—"Blow, Press, Burnish"—"Blow, Press, Burnish. . . ."

To Place the Sheet of Gold on the Gilder's Cushion

Open a package of glass gold. Inside is a booklet consisting of a cover with a rouged sheet of paper separating each leaf of gold. Holding the book in a horizontal position, turn the cover sheet and the tissue covering the top sheet of gold to the back of the package, leaving a slight overlap of the cover on the edge of the gold. DO NOT PUT YOUR HANDS OR FINGERS ON THE GOLD! With your thumb, pinch the overlap against the gold. Place the book, gold down, on top of the gilder's cushion. Release your hold on the gold, and gently lift off the book. The gold should now be flat on the cushion. If the gold should cling to the book instead of the cushion, put the tissue back over the gold and blow on it with a strong warm breath, discharging the static which holds the gold to the book. Fold the tissue back, make the overlap again and place the book on the cushion once more. The gold should now separate from the book.

To Cut the Gold

Press the gilder's knife firmly on the gold. Cut through with a slight sawing motion, but avoid cutting the cushion. To start, cut the gold into 1/2" squares. Experience will show what size works best for you.

If there is any oil on your knife the gold will adhere to it and be torn apart. Unless the knife is clean the whole sheet may be lost. To clean the knife, disengage it from the gold and fog it with your breath. Clean it vigorously several times with a clean cotton cloth or a paper towel or tissue. Repeat these steps until the knife cuts the gold neatly. Your hands are your worst enemy: no matter how clean they seem, keep them off the working ends of the tools.

Put the straw in your mouth and blow on the area where you will be placing the piece of gold. Blow from the throat, do not puff from the mouth, as you want warm moisture to form on the base. Blow slowly and evenly, about the length of a sigh, two or three times. With tweezers in the left hand holding a piece of gold by its edge, and a double layer of silk wrapped around the right thumb, blow and immediately lay the gold on that spot, pressing it down immediately with the silk, using a firm pressure. Then lift your thumb and silk off of the gold. Do not slide it off, as the gold may come with it. Replace the straw, drop the silk, and pick up the burnisher. Begin to burnish the gold, gently at first, until the gold becomes shiny. Then apply more pressure to polish it. Only practice can tell you how soon heavy pressure may be used. The goal is a bright mirror finish. (Remember—"Blow, Press, Burnish . . .")

A note of caution: Keep the straw clear of condensation by blowing through it sharply away from the work. If drops fall on the base, unnoticed, the gold and base will come apart during burnishing. If they

14. *London Hours of Rene d'Anjou, France, 1409*
Full frame borders dominated by acanthus interspersed with a few birds and flowers.

fall on the gold, subsequent layers will come off when applied, sometimes floating off. If this happens, use the tip of an absorbent paper towel or facial tissue to carefully draw off the moisture; then let it dry.

Replace the burnisher and pick up the large brush. Sweep off the excess gold. Use the magnifying glass to inspect the gold coverage to make sure that the area is completely covered.

When one layer of gold has been applied and burnished in a small area, repeat the process with another layer. Each layer of gold must be burnished before laying the next. In all, use two layers if double-weight gold is employed, and four layers if using single-weight gold.

As you finish a portion of the design, clean it by brushing off the excess gold, using the sharpened eraser (see photo 17) to remove gold that sticks to the paper, and to clean around the edges. Inspect the work carefully using the magnifying glass.

When some facility has been gained in laying and burnishing gold, move forward to laying down several pieces at a time. However, do not overlap the gold pieces as you press them on the gesso since any overlap burnishes off, thus wasting gold. Instead, align the pieces edge to edge. If you overlap in applying subsequent layers of gold without burnishing, there is always a danger of lifting the gold completely off the gesso. It is better to cover and finish a small area than to try to cover too much territory at once.

An alternate approach is to employ the burnisher, instead of the silk, to press down the gold. Blow on the gesso as above, pressing the gold down with the burnisher. The initial blow is often enough to lay two

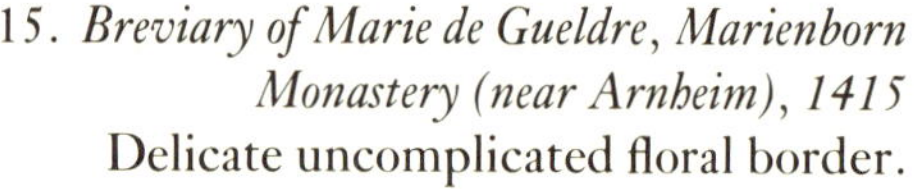

15. *Breviary of Marie de Gueldre, Marienborn Monastery (near Arnheim), 1415*
Delicate uncomplicated floral border.

or three layers of gold. Use caution; when employing this technique under what would normally be considered "ideal weather conditions," excessive blowing can soften the base too much. The edge of the burnisher could then mar the base irreparably.

Try not to burnish any ungilded gesso. This will inhibit its acceptance of the gold. In practice it is impossible to avoid this problem altogether. When the gold will not stick on such a polished area, gently scrape the surface of the base with a knife or scratch pen to remove the shine. Do not leave scratches on the base; the purpose is merely to retexture. Brush off the grit and proceed as usual.

If scratches are visible after gilding, scrape off the gold, repeat the smoothing process and regild the base. This is one reason why gesso should not be applied in a thin layer; if such corrections become necessary there would not be enough base remaining for gilding.

Secondly, there will be times when the base will have stubborn areas. It will resist the gold, or, having accepted one layer, both layers will lift off when another layer is applied. This can be a very frustrating experience. The fault could lie in one of the following.

1. The gesso itself was improperly ground.

2. During its application to the skin or paper, the gesso was not stirred often enough. As the base sits, the ingredients settle, with the heavier elements sinking to the bottom. If it was not stirred frequently between dips of the pen or brush, the gesso will be unbalanced.

3. The weather was too dry.

If none of these reasons apply, don't force the gold to such a spot. Such efforts will merely polish the gesso. Scrape and clean the gesso as described above. Wait a day or two. Blow again with a prolonged breath and put down the gold again. With the silk wrapped around the thumb, or, employing just the burnisher, press down on the gold with as much pressure as possible (sometimes standing helps to give more leverage). The gold should adhere.

PHOTOGRAPHS

The following close-up photographs portray, in the sequence of the work, the details of key steps in the development, application and gilding of gesso in the traditional manner.

1. *Rock sugar to be pulverized.*

2. *Powdered sugar, glue and bole mixed together.*

3. *Initial grinding: water added to part of gesso materials.*

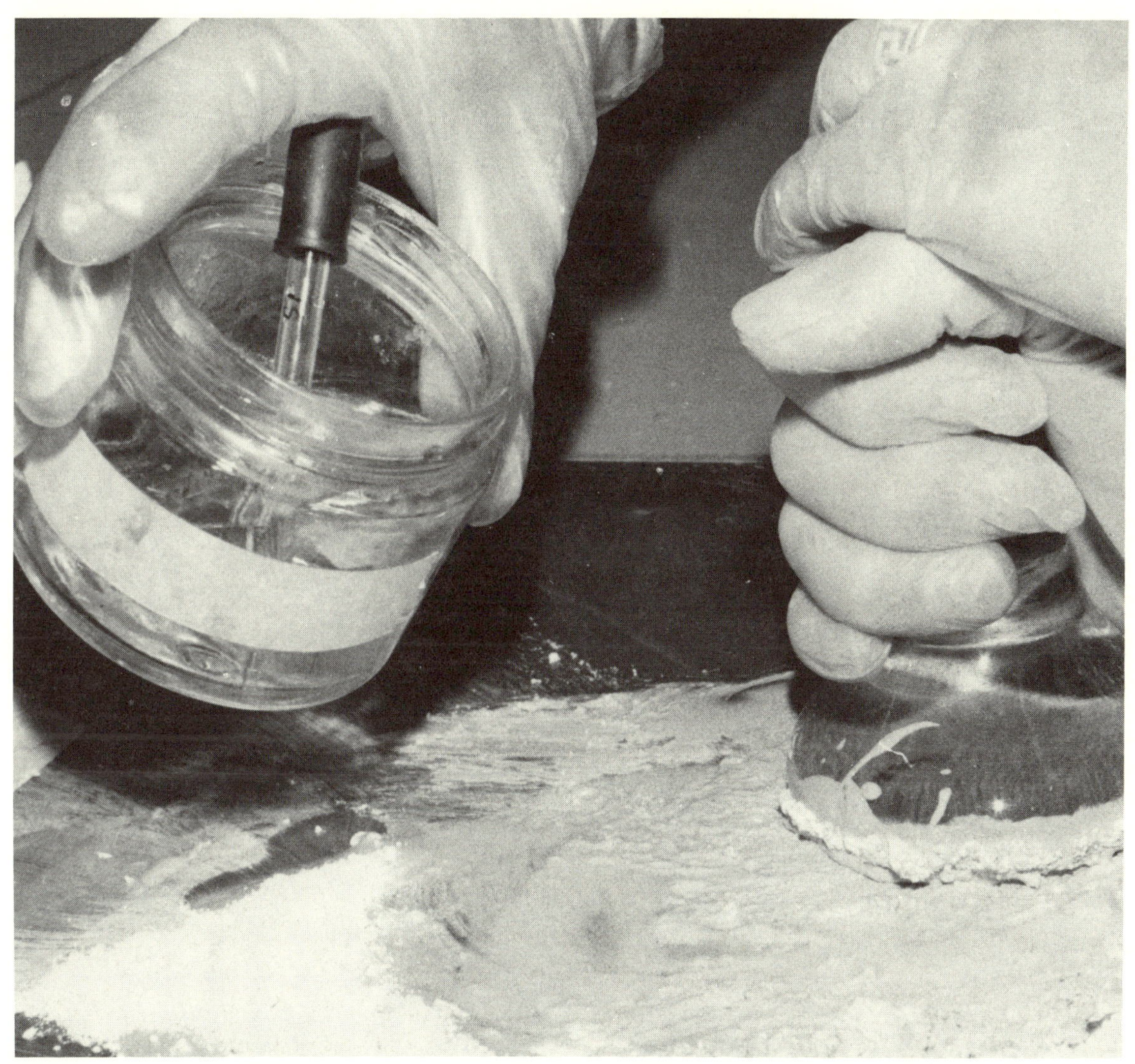

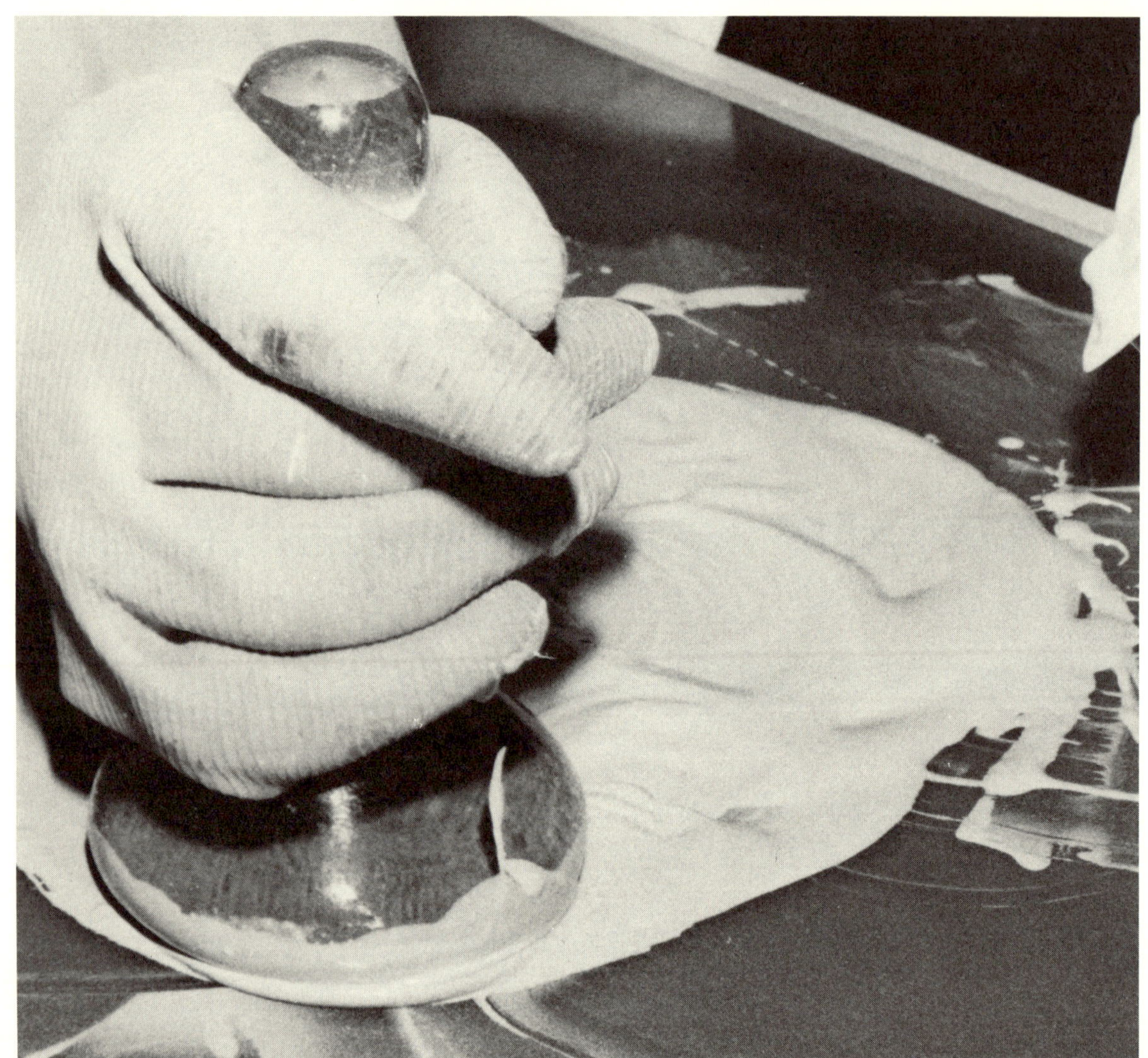

4. Initial grinding of gesso: part of measured white lead and slaked plaster pulled into mixture.

5. Final grinding: all materials added.

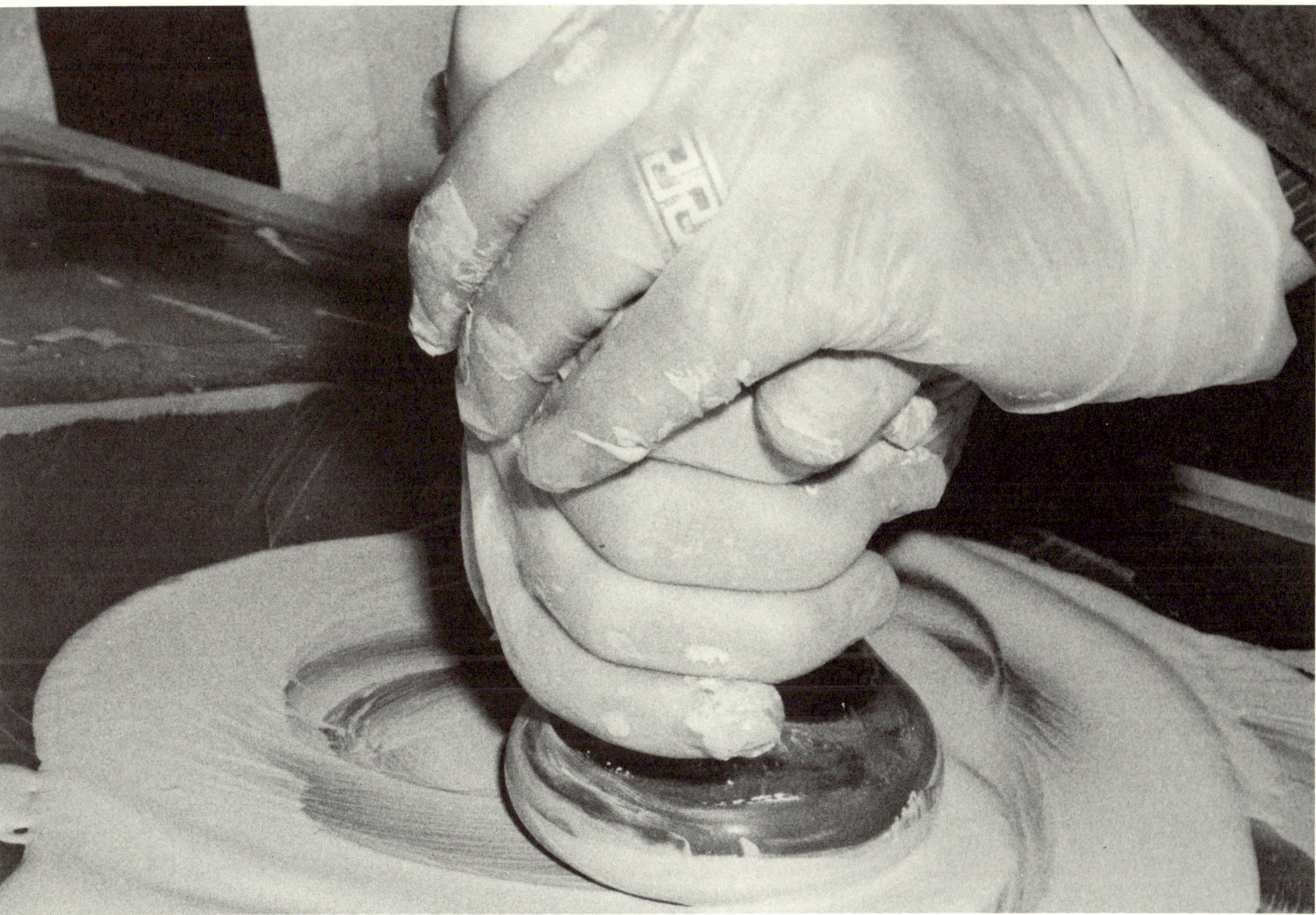

6. *Gesso ready to be made into patties.*

7. *Making small patties of gesso to be set aside to dry.*

8. *Dried gesso in shot glass.*

9. *Liquified gesso stirred with finger cot.*

10. *Application of reconstituted gesso.*

11. *Tools of the trade.*

12. *Gentle scraping to smooth the gesso.*

13. *Applying the gold leaf.*

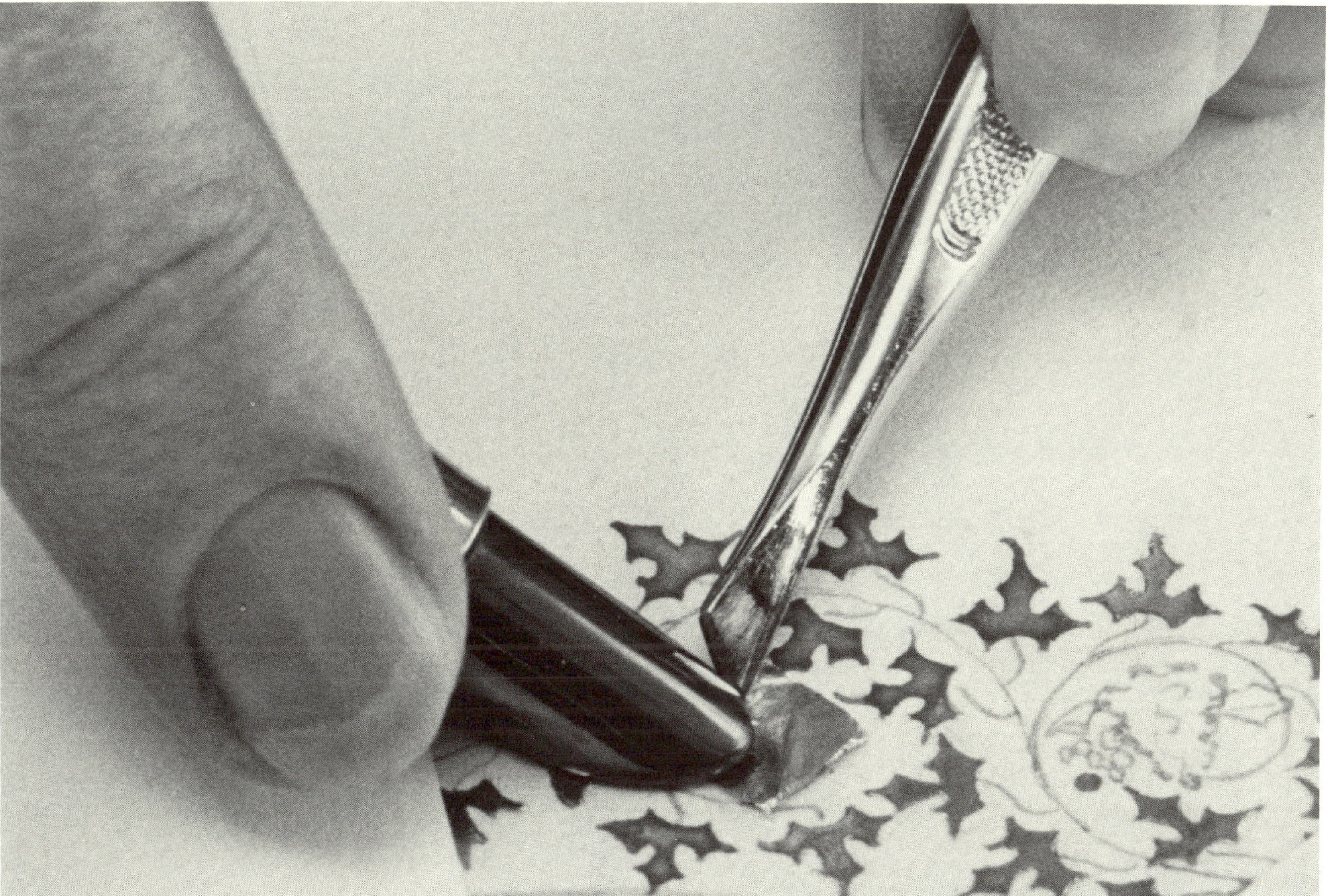

14. *Burnishing the gold.*

15. *Pushing up the edges of the gesso with a pencil burnisher.*

16. *Brushing off the excess gold.*

17. *Cleaning up with a sharpened ink eraser.*

18. *Defining edges with a scratch-nib. Following this final step, the entire work should be reburnished and brushed clean.*

Chapter Three
HYPLAR

EXPERIMENTING in the late 1960s, the calligrapher Ruth Josslin developed a unique technique for making a raised base which has become a viable alternative to gesso. This method employs Hyplar, which is the brand name of the gloss medium and varnish manufactured by M. Grumbacher, Inc. A comparable product with similar properties is Liquitex, manufactured by Binney & Smith. A petroleum product, the medium is a semi-thick, opaque, white liquid that dries clear. The primary advantage of this base is that is *always* works. However, Hyplar does have its limitations. It must be applied in multiple layers, and generally when dry it assumes the texture of the surface to which it has been applied. Over time the mirror finish of the gold will lose some of its brightness.

To build a raised base, Hyplar is applied in many thin coats. Each layer must dry completely before the next is applied, which, in turn, must be placed *exactly* over the previous coat. Checking it with a magnifying glass is the only sure way to accomplish this. Fresh Hyplar must be mixed for each layer of base. *Do not* use any base that has been sitting for much more than an hour. When Hyplar sits for any length of time, a film forms which must not be reincorporated by mixing. Even the slightest remixing allows bits of film to catch in the brush and, when the base is applied, causes blobs to appear which will dry as bumps.

TO MIX THE BASE

You will need:

Hyplar

Red watercolor

Distilled water

Eye dropper. For adding water to the base.

Small dish. The type ordinarily used for serving oriental sauces is best. It should be about 2" across the rim and 1/2" deep. It must have an absolutely smooth bottom area for even mixing.

Flat wooden toothpicks for mixing

After purchasing Hyplar, take care not to drop or roll it. *Do not shake it*; bubbles will form which can take weeks to rise. Over time, Hyplar develops a watery layer at the top of the container. Simply use a brush handle, or other appropriate tool, to carefully reincorporate the water. As it ages, the Hyplar will thicken in the container; this does no harm as it can be easily thinned with water when making the base.

1. Pour about 1/2 teaspoon of Hyplar into the dish. Add one or two drops of water with the eyedropper.

2. With the large end of the toothpick, pick up just enough red watercolor to tint the base pink (so it is visible). Slip the toothpick down the side of the dish and into the Hyplar. This method of entering the base helps to prevent bubbles. For the same reason, do not move the toothpick into and out of the base while mixing.

3. Stir with the toothpick, slowly and carefully in a circular fashion, until thoroughly mixed. If more water is needed, add it at the edge of the mixture and pull it in with the toothpick as you stir. When finished it will have the consistency of unwhipped cream. Check for bubbles with the magnifying glass and pull any that have developed out of the dish using a toothpick.

If the base dries in the mixing dish, loosen and lift it out with the tip of a knife.

61

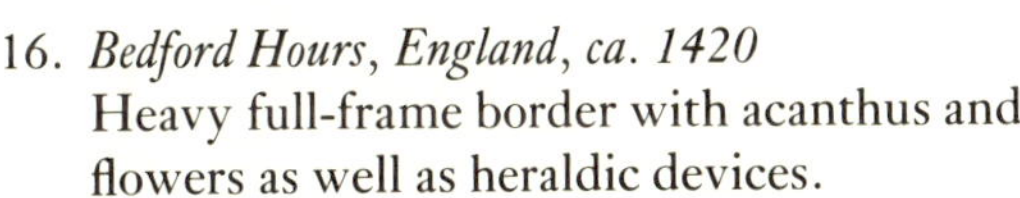

16. *Bedford Hours, England, ca. 1420*
Heavy full-frame border with acanthus and flowers as well as heraldic devices.

TO APPLY HYPLAR

A brief reminder before proceeding. To avoid creating more work for yourself, remember: first, calligraphy; second, gilding; and lastly, the painting.

You will need:

Mixed Hyplar

Prepared design. A final design transferred to the selected surface, gone over with diluted waterproof ink, and pencil marks erased. (See "Paper, Tracing" in Technical Notes.)

Large, smooth safety glass
Small brush
Magnifying glass
Slip sheets
Water jar for cleaning brush

Hyplar is applied using the puddle-pull method. Dip your brush into the base; pushing it down into the bottom will cause bubbles. Make a puddle with it on the paper or skin, pulling the base from it using short pulls. Make another puddle that connects with the pulled strokes. Continue in this manner, always keeping the base an even thickness, until the design is covered. While working, wash out the brush often. This base hardens in the bristles, causing them to spread, making the brush unmanageable and can result in the permanent loss of the tool.

1. With the glass centered to your body, apply Hyplar with the puddle-pull method. *Do not paint* with it. Discard unused Hyplar. Allow 24 hours drying time between each layer.

2. Subsequent layers of base should be mixed to a slightly thinner consistency than the original base. The final layer of base may be very thin. Before putting

down the final layer of Hyplar, be sure that you have allowed enough time in the day for application, drying and gilding. Always apply base with the magnifying glass in one hand. Check your work constantly. To determine readiness for gilding, let the base dry for 45 minutes, then blow on it with a straw; the base will fog over. If the fog remains on the base for 5 seconds before disappearing, the base is ready for gilding; if the fog stays longer, it is too wet; if it fogs and dissipates immediately, it is too wet or too dry.

Only put down as much of the final layer of Hyplar as you can gild before it dries. If so much area is prepared that the gilding cannot be accomplished in a single period of time, the ungilded area of base will dry, requiring recoating with fresh Hyplar. This part of the design would then be raised more than that previously gilded.

With Hyplar you may *not* go back and repair it when it is semi-wet. The cracks and indentations can be filled in after it has dried. If the surfaces still do not meet, fill them again and let dry. Then, put a thin layer of base over the entire area that has been repaired to make it even. Let each layer of base dry before putting down the next. If the base is correctly applied it will not be necessary to bother with repairs.

Remember to blow out the straw frequently or drops of moisture will fall on the base, causing a delay while that area dries again.

TO GILD HYPLAR

You will need:

Large, smooth safety glass
Glass gold
Gilder's cushion

17. *Hague Book of Hours, Flanders, 1454-5*
Free pen-work letter here introduces the text but may also appear as capitals within the text—either way a welcome relief from heavy decorative aspects of historiated and illuminated letters: I call these spider letters.

Knife, for gold
Tweezers
Plastic drinking straw. With 2" to 3" cut from the end.
Silk square
Burnisher
Large, soft brush
Scratch pen and holder
Sharpened ink eraser

Have the glass centered to the body with tools and materials arranged conveniently for use.

1. Blow on the base with the straw to fog the area. When the fog disperses in 5 seconds it is ready to gild.

2. With the tweezers holding a piece of gold in one hand, the straw in your mouth and silk wrapped around the opposite thumb, blow to fog the base. Immediately press the gold with the silk. Drop the silk and pick up the burnisher. Burnish lightly, gradually applying more pressure to polish it to a mirror finish. Brush off the excess gold with the large soft brush. (Remember the rhythm—"Blow, Press, Burnish. . . .")

3. Continue gilding and burnishing until you have applied 4 layers of single-weight gold, or two of double-weight. Sometimes the base, having been hit too hard in the burnishing, will show through in the high spots of contoured designs. Check for these spots with the magnifying glass and touch them up with more gold.

4. Clean off the excess with brush and sharpened ink eraser. Edge the design with the scratch pen and burnish again (See TO GILD GUM AMMONIAC, page 12.) As you edge, do not dig into the paper or skin surface any more than you must.

PRACTICING WITH HYPLAR

In addition to the puddle-pull technique, the use of Hyplar requires facility with the layering process. With geometric figures outlined (see PRACTICING WITH BASES, Page 4) and the Hyplar base mixed, put down one layer of base on each of the figures, using the puddle-pull method. Discard unused Hyplar. Let it dry for 45 minutes. Blow on the base with the straw. The base will fog over. If the fog remains on the base for 5 seconds before disappearing, the base is ready for gilding; if the fog stays longer it is too wet; if it fogs and dissipates immediately it is either too wet or too dry.

Gild the base by blowing on it through the straw, quickly pressing the gold on with the silk, and then burnish as on gesso. Brush off the excess gold and edge with the scratch pen. You now have a sample of one-layer appearance.

Next, draw a new set of designs, mix fresh Hyplar and apply one coat to each design. Allow them to dry completely (24 hours). Discard unused Hyplar; never use leftover base. Mix and apply a second coat to each, joining all edges exactly. After 45 minutes, blow on each with the straw to see if they are ready to gild. If the fog disappears in 5 seconds you may gild. You now have a sample of the two-layer appearance.

When you have finished these practice designs, do another set building as many layers as you like, always allowing each layer to dry for 24 hours before applying the next. When many layers of base have been applied, the final layers should be watery thin. This is how a base of Hyplar is raised.

If you wish to texture a design, such as the petals of a flower, put two layers of base over all of the design, letting the first dry before applying (with fresh base) the second. When that has dried, mix fresh base and lay it where you want emphasis on the flower. Do this using as many coats as desired, letting each dry to the point where fresh base can be laid without disturbing the previous layer. Allow to dry completely. Mix a final thin coat and cover the entire design. Let dry to the 5-second point and gild. As you gild this raised design, bear in mind that if the burnisher sticks, then it is still too wet. This often happens when many layers have been applied. Wait a bit longer to gild. As more layers are built up the drying time will increase beyond the initial 45 minutes.

If the base has developed cracks or indentations, or does not appear to be smoothly applied, it is due to not maintaining an even thickness of the base, using base that was too thick, or applying new base when the previous layer has not dried.

Chapter Four

EGG TEMPERA & GLAIR

THE COLORS that have endured in centuries-old manuscripts are remarkable for their brilliance. All painting of similar periods was executed with tempera or glair combined with pigment and either oil or water, making intense colors and forming a most durable film. However, the book had the preservatory advantage of being closed, preventing light and air from coming in contact with the ink, and gold.

Prior to the 1700s, artists had to grind their own pigment,[2] an enterprise not without hazard. Many pigments contained toxic "heavy metals," such as red and white lead (minium and ceruse); arsenic (orpiment) and mercury (cinnabar). The pigments were ground and reground, then, in combination with a solution of gum arabic or gum tragacanth as a binder, they were ground again. When used as watercolor, illuminators tempered the mixture with a solution of sugar or honey as a plasticizer, and then added tempera or glair; glair has also been used as a base for laying gold. A binder binds the pigment particles to themselves and attaches them to a ground; the plasticizer improves the brushing qualities and gives flexibility to the dried paint.

Some of the pigment sources during the period of book illumination include:[3,4]

Reds. Cinnabar (native mercuric sulfide); vermillion (manufactured mercuric sulfide); minium (red lead).

Blues. Ultramarine (originally made

---

[2]Ralph Mayer, *A Dictionary of Art Terms and Techniques* (New York, 1981), pp. 426-7.

[3]*De Arte Illuminandi* (New Haven, 1933), pp. 5-12.
[4]Daniel V. Thompson, *The Materials and Techniques of Medieval Painting* (New York, 1956), pp. 74-188.

18. *Le Livre de Coeur d'Amours Espris, France, 1457*
Example from a secular book showing full floral border and geometric sentence bars.

from lapis lazuli, now made artificially); turnsole blue (the turnsole plant produced this non-permanent blue which turned violet).

Greens. Terra verte (a native clay); verdigris (basic copper acetate); iris green (juice of purple iris, sometimes mixed with giallorino).

Rose. Extracted from Brazilwood and mixed with alum.

Yellows. Yellow ochre, raw sienna (native clays); various yellows from plants (turmeric root, rocket and dyers' weed).

Whites. Ceruse (white lead); calcined bones.

Blacks. Lamp black; vine twig charcoal; calcined ivory.

The development of commercial watercolor in the eighteenth century was a boon to the artist, freeing him from the chore and danger of making his own. These first watercolors were hard, dry cakes, embossed with the maker's trademark. With the addition of glycerin to the traditional combination of pigment, binder and plasticizer, the first marketable moist watercolors were created around 1835. The paste form of watercolor seen in stores today was developed about 1900. Standardization of permanent pigments in the United States (1942) and England (1957) has also benefited the artist by assuring an acceptable level of quality.

While the arduous task of pigment grinding is no longer necessary, the use of egg tempera and glair remain significant. To become familiar with them in their various combinations of both color and texture it is best to make a color wheel, a circular arrangement of the spectrum, using watercolors in different blends. The

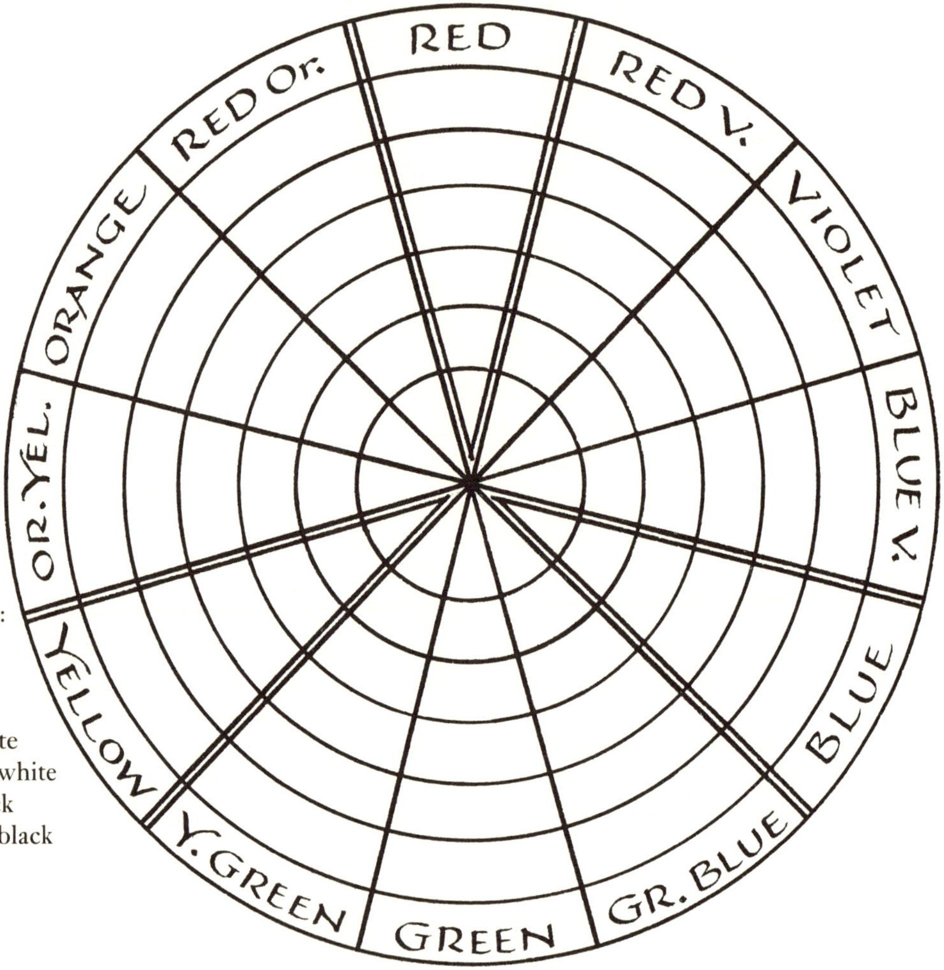

Figure 4. *Color wheel.*

From point of pie to outer edge:

1. Watercolor with water
2. Watercolor with glair
3. Watercolor with tempera
4. Watercolor with glair & white
5. Watercolor with tempera & white
6. Watercolor with glair & black
7. Watercolor with tempera & black

colors should be arranged in the order illustrated in Figure 4. Warm colors are in the half containing red and yellow, and cool colors are in the other half. Complementary colors are opposite one another.

Make an 8" or 9" circle on the paper with the compass. With pencil and straight edge, divide the circle into 12 or 16 pie-shaped pieces, depending on the number of colors you have. Make 6 progressively smaller circles inside the large one. Outside the large circle, number the divisions, indexing each for the mix of paint that will be put there. (Fig. 4.)

TO MAKE EGG TEMPERA AND GLAIR

You will need:

1 egg

Mixing bowl. Large enough to accommodate an egg beater

Egg beater

Distilled water

2 small jars with lids. 4 oz. baby food jars are good.

Paper towels

1. Break the egg in half. Separate the white into the bowl and the yolk onto the paper towel. Reserve one half of the shell.

2. With the egg beater, beat the egg white until it is very stiff. Fill the reserved shell with distilled water and pour it over the beaten white and set aside for 6 to 8 hours or overnight.

3. As the yolk air-dries on the paper towel the albumen that covers it will dry to a sort of crust in 1 to 2 hours. When it has dried sufficiently (so that it is no longer sticky) prick it with a pin, or a fingernail, and drain the contents into one of the small jars. Discard towel and yolk crust. Put the

lid securely on the jar and refrigerate. This is the egg tempera.

4. When the egg white has set the prescribed time, the froth on top will become dry and almost transparent. The bottom of the bowl will contain liquid. Drain this liguid into the second jar and discard the froth. Put a lid securely on the jar and refrigerate. This is the glair.

Traditionally, egg tempera is mixed with warm colors and glair is mixed with cool colors, but I like tempera in all of them, due to the rich quality it imparts to the paint. Cennini, in the fifteenth century, advised using only pale-colored yolks, but the color in an egg yolk, carotin, is fugitive and does not affect the dried paint.

Tempera does not store well. The yolk should be good for a week, provided it has not been out of the refrigerator for long periods of time. When the tempera deteriorates it develops a bad odor. If this occurs, discard the old tempera and make a fresh batch. Glair will keep longer, but it too decomposes with age and it is better to make fresh than tolerate the odor.

TO USE TEMPERA AND GLAIR

You will need:

Watercolors. Tube variety, at least 12 different colors, similar to those suggested in Fig. 4.

Palette. White, with seven or more divisions.

Small brush

Egg tempera

Glair

Toothpicks. Flat wooden ones to mix the paint.

Eye dropper

Distilled water. To thin paint and clean brush.

19. *Hours of Alfonso of Aragon, Duke of Calabria, Naples, 1480*
Interlace patterns reappear in this and other pieces dating from Italian Renaissance—the pattern now referred to as "vermicelli."

Jar, with water. To thin paint and clean brush.

1. Place some of one color in each of 7 of the separators in the palette; each will be mixed differently. Use a toothpick to stir the colors. (If a brush is used for blending, bubbles will form.)

2. Add tempera to the watercolor in a 1-to-1 ratio, with a drop or two of water to thin. Add more water if the mix does not spread evenly. Glair is mixed with the watercolor in the same way, although it may not require thinning.

It is a good practice to make a test patch on an extra piece of paper to make certain the paint is flowing properly. When applied, the color should cover with a solid look; the brush should not leave streaks with the paper showing through. Note that watercolors are transparent, and unless mixed with white will remain so. Tempera and glair, especially when covering large areas of a design, often need to be applied using the puddle-pull method employed in laying gilding bases, rather than "painted." Tempera dries with a slightly raised surface.

If it becomes necessary to change a color when working with skin, just let it dry, scrape it off, then repaint. This will also work with paper, however more pigment remains behind, staining the surface, which can generally be covered when repainting.

3. Continue mixing paint in the combinations suggested for making a color wheel until you have the 7 mixtures ready to apply. Paint in the colors; wash out the palette and proceed to mix the same combinations with a new color.

20. *Soane Hours, Flemish School, ca. 1500* An example of the last definitive style of manuscript illumination distinctive for borders with realistic oversized design elements.

Technical Notes

GESSO SOTTILE

In a bucket that will comfortably hold one gallon of water, with room for stirring, put:

1/2 pound plaster of Paris
1 gallon distilled water

Add the plaster of Paris to the water, stirring for 30 minutes (so that the plaster will not set up in the bottom of the pail). Set aside, covering the pail loosely with the sheet of butcher paper, or some other porous material that will permit evaporation and keep it free of dust. Store in a cool place away from direct light. Stir every day for two or three minutes for 30 days. (If it begins to smell rotten, pour off as much of the water as you can, without losing any of the plaster. Replace with the same amount of fresh distilled water.) Do not stir the day before draining so that the plaster can settle more completely.

To drain, first prepare a blotting area with a thick layer of newspaper and cover it with a plain white blotter. Also line a colander (one with a funnel shape is best) with a coffee filter or paper towels. Then, using a ladle or a tin can, or by carefully pouring, remove as much water as possible without disturbing the settled plaster. Pour the remaining water and plaster into the lined colander and let it drain.

Spread the well-drained plaster onto the blotter and let it sit for 20 minutes. Transfer the plaster by the tablespoon to waxed paper, forming small cakes. Dry in a dust-free environment for two days to a week, depending on the weather. Stored in a dry place, in a clean container, it will keep indefinitely.

GILDER'S CUSHION

To construct a gilder's cushion you will need:

A wooden block. Approximately 7" square, 3/4" to 1" thick.

A piece of heavy suede about 9" square. Which you can find in the scraps of any leather shop.

Cotton padding, thumb tacks, and hammer

Cover the top of the wooden block with the cotton padding in an even layer.

Stretch the leather down snugly, suede-side up, and tack to the edges of the block, using the hammer to secure the tacks. (Fig. 5.)

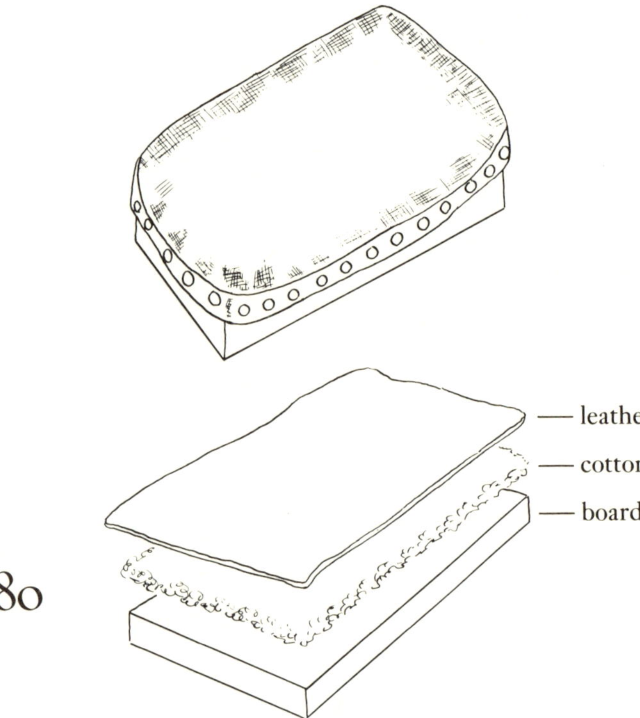

Figure 5. *How to make gilder's cushion.*

GOLD LEAF VARIETIES

Single Weight Gold

Glass gold: 22k to 23k supplied in two grades: glass gold, the best quality, and signboard or surface gold, which is slightly cheaper and contains small imperfections. It is best to use glass gold.

Lemon gold: 18k, is lighter in color than glass gold.

Pale gold: 16k, is lighter in color than the lemon gold.

White gold: 13k to 14k, is an alloy of half gold and half silver. Quite silver in color, it will tarnish slightly over time.

Patent gold: comes with the sheet of gold affixed to a tissue, is easy to handle and is pre-burnished. Used primarily on gum ammoniac base it will not maintain a high polish.

Double Weight Gold

Due to its weight, less of it is required for gilding. It is difficult to find. In England, a special illuminating gold leaf of 24k is produced.

Booklets of gold leaf come from many manufacturers. They are packaged under different names, such as "XX Deep Glass Gold," "XX Deep Gold,"

"XX Deep Gold Leaf" and simply, "Gold Leaf." Most of these can be purchased at a graphic art supply store or a paint store. The word "glass" usually indicates the best quality of gold leaf.

GOLD/SHELL

This form of gold is made from beaten gold leaf and is usually sold in tablet form. It can be burnished but does not take a high polish.

To use shell gold: Dampen a brush with water, and with the wet brush proceed to dampen a corner of the tablet. Transfer the gold caught in the wet brush to a clean area beside the table. Continue to work up the gold and water until you have a small puddle that is well saturated with the gold. Then use it like paint, or thinned a bit, it can be used as an ink. Alternatively, the gold can be tempered with a gum arabic solution and used to paint on top of colors and make delicate lines. Be miserly about how much you mix at a time. It is *very* expensive to use.

GUM ARABIC

To make a solution from purchased gum arabic powder: In the top of a double boiler, over simmering water, dissolve 1 measure of gum arabic powder in 2 measures distilled water. Stir constantly, adding more water until a viscous solution is obtained (it will look like clear syrup). Put in a clean jar, with tight lid. It will keep indefinitely.

PALLADIUM LEAF

Is made from a silvery metal of the platinum family and costs more than gold leaf. Palladium is darker than silver leaf and has a slight brownish color cast. It does not tarnish. Very expensive and hard to find.

PAPER/TRACING

To transfer a design, using tracing paper: First, square the paper, mark margins and a center line on the working surface identical to those on the tracing paper. These are used to align the design accurately for the transfer. Graphitize the back of the paper with a very soft pencil. Rub off the excess with cotton or a paper tissue. Repeat the process. Place the paper with the graphitized side on the working surface and tape it securely in place with drafting tape. With a hard pencil trace the design. When completely transferred, remove the paper. Using diluted waterproof ink, go over the entire design with a crowquill pen. Carefully erase any pencil marks remaining and you have the design down permanently. The ink will not run when wet with paint or base.

An alternate approach is to put a fresh piece of tracing paper over the tracing paper on which you have made the design, and trace it off. Proceed with the graphitizing as above, using the fresh tracing. This protects the original design from wear and tear, preserving it for future use.

An historical approach used by the medieval illuminator was to use a stencil, made by drawing a design on animal skin, then piercing the design with tiny holes. The design was then transferred by "pouncing" the stencil with colored powder or charcoal dust. A grid was often drawn on these stencils to facilitate the enlargement or reduction of the design.

QUILLS

"Dutch method of preparing goose quills for writing: The process consists in immersing the quill when plucked from the wing of the bird into water almost boiling; to leave it there till it becomes sufficiently soft to compress it, turning it on its axis with the back of the blade of the knife. This kind of friction, as well as the immersion in water to be continued till the barrel of the quill be transparent, and the membrane as well as the greasy kind of covering, be entirely removed; it is immersed a last time to render it perfectly cylindrical, which is performed with the index finger and thumb; it is then dried in a gentle temperature."[5]

SILVER LEAF

Should not be used for gilding because it tarnishes badly when exposed to air.

VELLUM

To prepare the skin you will need:

Pounce (pumice powder). Which is used to remove grease and give a mat surface.

Sandarac. It must be ground to a fine powder. Makes the ink blacker and produces sharp edges. It also gives tooth.

Sandpaper, *400-grit*. 250-grit garnet if the flesh

---

[5]Peter Brown, Pub. *The Repository of Arts and Sciences*, Edinburgh, 1838. p. 90-91.

side of a skin, other than slunk, is used.

Always use the hair side of the skin, as it is the best. Work for a surface that is non-greasy and slightly velvety. (The pen will flatten the pile, making a trough in which the ink and color will sit.)

On fine skins, such as slunk calfskin, there is no need for sandpaper. Pounce rubbed on with a cotton rag, or a very light sprinkle of ground sandarac, rubbed on and brushed off is sufficient. However, on the hair side of a heavier skin, dust on the pounce liberally and rub it in with a block covered with 400-grit sandpaper. Do this until the surface is non-greasy and slightly velvety. Dust on a little of the sandarac, which has been previously ground to a powder, and rub in with the same block. Clean the skin off with a brush or a piece of skin. Proceed cautiously, as it is easy to get too much sandarac down. It is hard, if not impossible to remove.

250-grit garnet sandpaper is used only to smooth the flesh side of a heavy piece of skin. The primary sanding would be performed with the 250-grit, and then it would be finished with the 400-grit sandpaper, using a circular motion.

Erasures can be made with a knife by lifting the ink or paint carefully from the skin without digging into the skin itself. Never work in one direction alone, because the object is to restore the nap of the surface.

Take care that none of the grit from the pounce or sandarac gets under the skin as you work. The area under the skin must be kept absolutely free of particles or you may rub a hole in it over the spots where they are lodged.

Glossary

Armenian bole: Also known as jeweler's rouge, Lemnos earth and terra sigillata, bole is a naturally occurring combination of hydrated iron and alumninum oxides. Used with gesso to impart color and polish, it is also hygroscopic.

Brush, large soft: Used for cleaning and brushing off excess gold. I suggest Grumbacher brushes 1/2" (4116), 3/4" (55 Meissonier) # (4020), or any make that matches in size and softness.

Brush, small: It must have a fine point (I use a Grumbacher #0, Series #178) or Winsor Newton #1 series 233). Used to apply base and paint. May be found in most art supply stores.

Burnisher, hematite: Hematite (or haematite; its traditional name is bloodstone) burnishes all bases and is far superior to agate in polish performance. Agate is *not* satisfactory for gesso.

Dish, small: Used for mixing Hyplar, it should be about 2" across the rim, 1/2" deep, and with a smooth bottom. Oriental sauce dishes are perfect for this.

Distilled water: Used for mixing gesso and other bases as well as cleaning tools and mixing colors. It is particularly necessary when working with vellum to reduce the possibility of mold and microorganisms. Unmentionable things may grow on skin if the water is not distilled. Found in local supermarkets.

Drafting tape: Like masking tape but not as sticky. Available in art and engineering supply stores.

Erasers: A *green* plastic artist-type eraser, such as that made by Farber. Gum erasers are not suitable due to their sulphur content. May be found in art supply stores.

A sharpened pencil-shaped ink eraser, for cleaning up flecks of gold from the finished work.

Eye dropper: Used for transferring water to mixtures, and for measuring parts by drops when making small quantities, such as waterproof ink.

Finger cots: Thin latex finger guards used to protect an individual finger when mixing gesso and gum ammoniac. Often available from drugstores, or a laboratory supply.

Fish glue: A component of gesso contributing binding and adhesion. It is prepared from the heads, bones and skins of fish. The glue manufactured from the swim sounds, or air bladders of certain fish, including sturgeon and hake, is called isinglass and is very near pure collagen. Seccotine is a common brand of fish glue available to calligraphers.

Gesso sottile: Plaster of Paris, slaked for 30 days with daily stirring; dry and store until needed. Preparation instructions included in Technical Notes.

Gilder's cushion: A slightly raised pillow on which to cut and lay gold. This may be purchased or you may make your own, which is considerably cheaper and just as satisfactory. Instructions included with Technical Notes.

Gilder's knife: You may purchase a knife specifically designed for this purpose or find and use any very sharp knife with a blade 7" to 8" in length, having a straight, not a curved, cutting edge. This knife should never be used for anything but cutting gold, and must be thoroughly cleaned before use.

Glass: 2 large pieces of 1/4" safety glass, approximately 17" x 22". Tape them around the edges to prevent injury to self and property.
#1 glass (for making gesso) should be:

Thick—so grinding can be accomplished without breakage, and so it will not "give" when pressure is applied.

Rough surfaced—enabling elements to be ground on it. You can have this piece sandblasted at your friendly neighborhood glass store.

Large—to provide enough room to work comfortably.

#2 glass (for laying base, gilding and painting) should be:

Thick and hard—to allow proper leverage for burnishing without breakage, and so it will not "give" when pressure is applied.

Large—to provide enough room to work comfortably.

Smooth—to provide the proper surface to burnish on.

Glass provides a cool surface which slows evaporation of the moisture breathed onto the various bases.

Glass muller: Is made of glass with a hand grip that tapers out to an approximate 3" circular flat base. Used to grind the materials for making gesso. (Fig. 6)

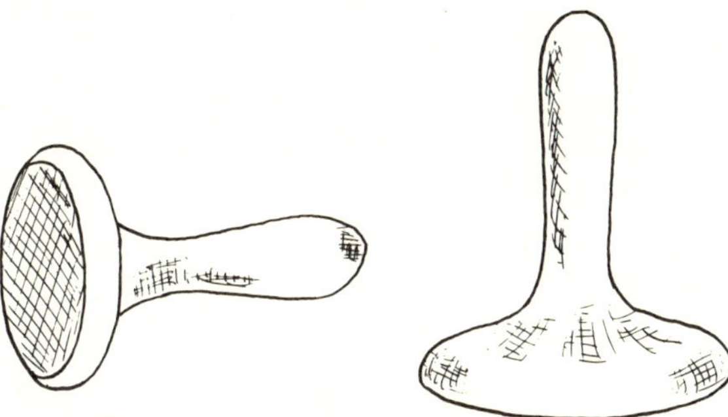

Figure 6. *Glass muller.*

Gold leaf: Comes packaged in booklets containing 25 sheets. Each sheet of gold measures 3⅜ x 3⅜". Varieties detailed in Technical Notes.

Gum ammoniac: Is not a true gum, but a resin collected from *Ferula*, a very large genus of Old World plants of the carrot family normally used medicinally. A base for laying gold leaf.

Gum arabic: A gum of the *Mimosaceous* plants; the best grades come from the *Acacia Senegal*. It is soluble in hot water and used in solution as the medium in watercolor and gum tempera. Gum arabic solutions are often available in art supply stores, but the gum powder may also be purchased from chemical companies; sometimes drugstores have it on hand. Instructions for preparation included in Technical Notes.

Hyplar: A brand name of gloss medium and varnish base produced by M. Grumbacher, Inc. (Liquitex, manufactured by Binney and Smith, is the brand name for a similar product.) Available in most art supply stores.

Magnifying glass: The hand-held type, with a diameter of 2" to 3", is best. You will use this constantly. Never work without one. Can be purchased in department stores, art supply stores, etc.

Measuring spoons: Standard kitchen variety, used for measuring materials, usually by parts.

Nibs: Springy, with a fine point (Brause #66EF recommended), and a larger nib with the same characteristics (such as Hunt's mapping nibs). Copperplate nibs are generally good if they are not so stiff they impede the flow of base or injure the surface of the vellum or paper.

Crowquill, which is used for outlining. Available at art supply shops.

Scratch, for edging your bases. Also carried at art supply shops.

Nylon hosiery: Used for straining gum ammoniac. Dynel, crepeline or fine-weave silk may also be used.

Palette: White, with seven or more mixing dishes. May be purchased at art supply stores.

Paper, for gilding: Always use an acid-free (neutral pH) hard-surfaced (cold-pressed) 100% cotton or high rag content paper with some weight to it.

Paper, tracing: Draft your designs on tracing paper so that good paper or vellum will not get messed up or destroyed in preliminary work.

Paper, glassine: Used to assist in the application of gold to gum ammoniac. Booklets of gold leaf usually come in glassine packets. Can be found in engineering and art supply stores.

Pen holders: small-sized one to hold the crowquill nib and a standard-sized holder for the scratch nib.

Parchment: See Vellum.

Pen knife: Employed to cut quills and to level your gesso base. A snap-blade knife (such as made by *Olfa*) may also be used.

Pencils: You will need two, one hard and one very soft. Used to draw and transfer designs.

Pounce: A fine resinous powder, usually a mix of sandarac and pumice or cuttlefish bone used to prepare paper and vellum for drawing and writing. The name also refers to a fine powder of charcoal or chalk used to transfer stencil patterns.

Quill pen: This is not necessary but if you have one, use it for laying and writing with gum ammoniac and gesso base. If you can not cut a quill, find someone who can; maybe they will do it for you!

Rock sugar: A component of gesso, it is hygroscopic and contributes elasticity to gesso.

Sandarac: A resin from the alerce tree, used to give "tooth" to paper or vellum surfaces. It also makes ink appear darker.

Shot glass: Used for blending the prepared gesso with distilled water. It should be the standard "shot" (1½ oz.) glass so that the bottom can be easily touched with a finger on the inside.

Silk: A piece 12" square, finely woven, light weight and extremely soft (such as an old head scarf) is needed. In pressing the gold down, the pattern of the fabric's weave becomes imprinted on the surface. Since this must be burnished away, using silk with a heavy weave creates more work. The material *must* be silk.

Slip sheets: Pieces of paper which mask all but the immediate work area.

Spatulas: Those made of bone, because of their natural curve, comfortable grip, specific design and texture are the best. They are also quieter and therefore easier on the nerves. Unfortunately, bone spatulas are not commercially available and would have to be made by hand. One acceptable substitute is a plastic bench or dough scraper which should measure at least 3" across. Metal spatulas should not be used while grinding since some pigments may be stained by the metal. A small metal spatula (like a sandwich spreader) is used for transferring the wet gesso mixture to a surface on which it can dry. It can be found in any kitchenware department.

Straw: A plastic drinking straw with 2" to 3" cut from the end. It is used to moisten the gilding bases immediately before laying the gold. Some people use a piece of rolled up blotter, which helps to control the condensation and dripping problems.

Surgical gloves: Used to protect the hands and to minimize direct contact with the white lead. Available in paint, art, surgical and dental supply stores, and drugstores.

Toothpicks: Use the flat wooden variety for stirring and mixing.

Tweezers: Only practical tool for handling gold leaf.

Vellum: Your choice will probably be between

slunk calf skin and manuscript calf skin. The latter can be thick, stiff and awkward to use, while the former is thin and quite lovely in feel and texture. Skin may be ordered from several outlets and some suppliers will, on request, send samples. A whole skin of manuscript vellum is much larger, and costs less, than a whole skin of slunk. Both can be purchased in pre-cut pieces.

Skin has a translucent quality that cannot be matched by any paper. If the surface is properly prepared it will give sharpness to the calligraphy and design, help to maintain evenness of color and ink, and give enough resistance (tooth) to prevent slipping or skating of the pen.

Watercolor: Use the tube variety of Grumbacher or Winsor-Newton. Stay away from non-permanent colors, such as vermillion and Van Dyke brown. Have a good selection on hand including ultramarine, cobalt blue, cadmium red, cadmium yellow (light and medium), terra verte, chrome oxide, yellow ochre, raw sienna, burnt umber, black and white. When mixing colors together stay with the same brand; sometimes colors of different brands do not combine well. Can be purchased at any art supply store.

Waterproof ink: Raw sienna color. Dilute it with 5 parts water to 1 part ink. It is used to outline designs after the transfer to paper or vellum. It can be purchased in art supply stores.

White lead: A component of gesso giving bulk, polish and malleability. WARNING: THIS IS A CUMULATIVE POISON. Wash hands thoroughly after using. Do not swallow it or breathe its dust. Keep brush tips *out of your mouth.*

Bibliography & Resources

BIBLIOGRAPHY

Alexander, J.J.G. *The Decorated Letter.* New York: George Braziller, Inc., 1978.

Anderson, Donald M. *The Art of Written Forms.* New York: Holt, Rinehart and Winston, 1969.

Bersch, Josef. *The Manufacture of Earth Colours.* Translated from the 3rd German edition by Charles Salter. London: Scott, Greenwood and Son, 1921.

Cennini, Cennino D'Andrea. *Il Libro Dell Arte (The Craftsman's Handbook).* Translated by Daniel V. Thompson, Jr. New York: Dover, 1960. Reprint of 1933 Yale University Press edition.

De Arte Illuminandi. Translated by Daniel V. Thompson, Jr. and George Heard Hamilton, from the Latin of Naples ms. XIII. E. 27. New Haven, CT: Yale University Press, 1933.

Diringer, David. *The Book Before Printing.* New York: Dover Publications, Inc., 1982. Reprint of 1952 edition; originally published as *The Hand-Produced Book*, London: Hutchinson's Scientific and Technical Publications.

Doerner, Max. *The Materials of the Artist.* Translated by Eugen Neuhaus. New York: Harcourt, Brace and World, 1962.

Lehmann-Haupt, Helmutt. *The Gottingen Model Book.* Columbia, MO: University of Missouri Press, 1978.

Mayer, Ralph. *A Dictionary of Art Terms and Techniques.* New York: Harper and Row, 1969.

McCann, Michael. *Artist Beware.* New York: Watson-Guptill, 1979.

Scheller, Richard W. *A Survey of Medieval Model Books.* Haarlem, The Netherlands: De Erven F. Bohn N.V., 1963. (Available from University Microfilms, Ann Arbor, MI.)

Theophilus, Presbyter. *On Divers Arts.* Translated by John G. Hawthorne and Cyril Stanley Smith. New York: Dover, 1979. Reprint of 1963 University of Chicago Press edition.

Thompson, Daniel V., Jr. "The DeClarea of the So-Called 'Anonymus Bernensis'." *Technical Studies in the Field of Fine Arts*, I:1 (July 1932) pp. 8-19.

———"Liber de Coloribus Illuminatorium Sive Pictorium from Sloane Ms. No. 1754." *Speculum*, I:3 (July 1926) pp. 280-307.

———*Materials and Techniques of Medieval Painting*. New York: Dover Publications, Inc., 1956. Reprint of 1936 Allen and Unwin edition.

———*Practice of Tempera Painting*. New York: Dover Publications, Inc., 1962. Reprint of 1936 Yale University Press edition.

Thompson, R. M. "The Library of Bury St. Edmonds Abbey in the Eleventh and Twelfth Centuries." *Speculum*, 47:4 (October 1972) pp. 617-645.

Toch, Maximillian. *The Chemistry and Technology of Paints*. New York: D. Van Nostrand, 1925. 3rd edition.

Tymms. W. R. and Wyatt, M. D. *The Art of Illuminating*. London: Day and Son, Ltd., 1861.

Wehlte, Kurt. *Materials and Technology of Paints*. Translated by Ursus Dix. New York: D. Van Nostrand Co., 1975. 3rd edition.

RESOURCES

Calligraphy and Gilding Supplies

Calligrafree
43 Ankara Ave.
Brookside, OH 45309

Nancy Ouchida Studio & Shop
2513 A Ocean Park Blvd.
Santa Monica, CA 90405

Pendragon
2643 N. Kimball
Chicago, IL 60647
(312) 278-0677

Pentalic Corp.
132 West 22nd St.
New York, NY 10011

Daniel Smith, Inc.
4130 1st Ave. S.
Seattle, WA 98134

George M. Whiley, Ltd.
Victoria Road, Ruislip
Middlesex, HA4 OLG ENGLAND
(For double gold)

Vellum

William Cowley
100 Caldecote St.
Newport Pagnell
Bucks, MK16 ODB ENGLAND

This book was designed by Charles Lehman, set in Centaur and Janson typefaces by Irish Setter of Portland, Oregon, and printed on 55# Glatfelter B-16 by Malloy Lithographing, Inc., of Ann Arbor, Michigan. Photographs were produced by Herman Grafe, and line drawings were made by Joyce Grafe.